DATE DUE

DISCARD

DEMCO 38-296

The Look of

HORROR

Scary Moments
from Scary Movies

COURAGE
BOOKS

An imprint of
RUNNING PRESS
Philadelphia, Pennsylvania

The Look of

HORROR

Scary Moments from Scary Movies

By

Jonathan Sternfield

Photographs from the Kobal Collection

One of the horror genre's most celebrated actors in his most famous role: Boris Karloff as the creature in Frankenstein *(see pp. 10-11).*

Whatis it with scary movies? Why are horror films some of the most popular movies ever? Perhaps it is that horror is sensational by nature. It takes viewers to unimaginable places, introduces them to fantastic beings, and forces them to watch the unwatchable. With its nail-biting suspense and alternating moments of terror and relief, a horror movie provides a truly cathartic release from the real tensions of everyday life.

"To show that, unconsciously, we all live in fear—that is the genuine horror," said Jacques Tourneur, director of the effective *Cat People* (1942). "Many people are constantly prey to a kind of fear they don't wish to analyze. When the audience, sitting in a darkened room, recognizes his own insecurity in the characters in the film, then you can show unbelievable situations in the certain knowledge that the audience will follow you."

Today, the "audience will follow" horror filmmakers, thanks in part to an arsenal of cinematic magic tricks. But horror wasn't always synonymous with special effects. In its silent beginnings, it concentrated on evoking ominous moods, and telling eerie tales. Thomas Edison's studio made a silent *Frankenstein* in 1910, but it wasn't until *The Cabinet of Dr. Caligari* in 1919 that a substantial horror film was created. The German *Caligari* forged a new path for all film, tangibly creating a subjective reality through distorted sets and odd camera angles. Here too was the genre's introduction to a triad of characters that would become horror archetypes, three individuals who would interact and keep the terror escalating through decades of scary movies: the mad scientist, his slave-monster, and the beautiful damsel in distress.

During the 1920s, Lon Chaney began to influence

Hollywood's idea of horror, giving memorable performances as very human freaks of nature in *The Hunchback of Notre Dame* (1923) and *The Phantom of the Opera* (1925). The 1920s also saw an emigration of German horror film specialists to Hollywood. Among them was Carl Laemmle, Jr., who, at Universal Studios, would lead Hollywood into the 1930s—the Golden Age of Horror—creating such legends as Boris Karloff and Bela Lugosi. In those days, the heroes were usually American, the settings and villains usually European.

The 1940s saw the humanization of horror, when ordinary people became monsters. *The Wolf Man* (1941) was one of the first evocations of this treatment. Meanwhile Tourneur's *Cat People* saw the horrific possibilities of suggestion, keeping the menace just out of sight while strongly indicating its presence through shadow or sound.

The real horror of Hiroshima marked a turning point in the genre. Americans began to fear the possible consequences of unbridled scientific experimentation, and consequently movie screens came to be dominated by the products of such investigations—giant spiders (*Tarantula*, 1955), for example, and mutant people (*The Fly*, 1958). On another front, *Invasion of the Body Snatchers* (1956) held a mirror up to the nation and showed it a version of 1950s conformity carried to the extreme. The 1950s also saw the rise of the teen market, and Hollywood was quick to retool its standard fare, creating the classic *I Was a Teenage Werewolf* (1957) and *I Was a Teenage Frankenstein* (1957) and showing teens saving the day in *The Blob* (1958).

The genre took another major turn in 1960 with the release of Alfred Hitchcock's *Psycho*. Here was a story of a sweet mama's boy, Norman Bates (Anthony Perkins), who the audience grows to like before it realizes that he is a cold-blooded murderer. Murderers are much like you and me, Hitchcock seems to be saying; more and more, we resemble the monster. The 1960s also saw a Gothic horror film revival, with several studios making and remaking spooky stuff in ghoulish living Technicolor. Now blood and gore could be shown in a nauseating palette of hues. In Britain, Gothic was the domain of the Hammer studio. In the United States, it was in the hands of Boris Karloff, Peter Lorre, and Vincent Price on the screen, and the very imaginative, fast-working Roger Corman behind the camera at American International Pictures.

From the end of the 1960s through the 1970s, there arose a countercultural horror, a refocusing of the genre within us. It began with Roman Polanski's *Rosemary's Baby* (1968), ran through the real-life Manson murders and political assassinations, and right into *The Exorcist* (1973), in which the ultimate evil comes to live in an innocent 12-year-old girl. *The Exorcist* marked the emergence of stomach-wrenching special effects, and from that moment on, horror films have been much messier—but also more believable. Director Steven Spielberg, for example, capitalized on the newly awakened frenzy for gore with his graphic shark attacks in *Jaws* (1975). This vivid and bloody narrative, which won Oscars for best sound, editing, and score, continues to be the top-grossing horror film of all time.

Predating *Jaws* were the gore, or "splatter," films that came into vogue, as much for their sheer outrageousness as for their depiction of evil. George Romero's *Night of the Living Dead* (1968), which depicts gleeful cannibalism, and Tobe Hooper's *The Texas Chainsaw Massacre* (1974) both contributed to a new and horrifying tangent within the genre.

As horror films have become more explicit in their violence and brutality, some industry observers have found cause for concern. Do these nightmarish visions infect our minds? Do they *create* crime or offer a cleansing release? How far will we let them go? These questions remain unresolved. But this much is clear: with their special effects trickery, dimensional sound and emotional orchestration through music, modern horror

Introduction

films in the hands of masters like John Carpenter (*Halloween* and *Christine*) can take audiences cartwheeling through an eternity's worth of terror. With their Oscar-winning visual effects and art direction, films like *Alien* (1979) can propel us into the creepy uncertainties of outer space.

Here then are 70 of the great—and not so great—ones, a ghoulish gallery of monsters, aliens, murderers, maniacs, mad doctors, creatures, bad and weird kids, ghosts, demons, and others too odd to classify. In words and pictures, their stories come alive, projecting scary moments from scary movies, transferring that look of horror . . . to you, the reader. Like the tingler, that nasty, crab-like creature that feeds on fear and severs the spine unless we cry out in terror, horror films force themselves upon us, terrorizing us for the fun of it.

But it must be obvious by now. We asked for it.

Monsters

Clearly Elsa Lanchester is not thrilled by the idea of romance with a monster in Bride of Frankenstein *(1935).*

Frankenstein

Mary Shelley's 1818 novel, *Frankenstein, or a Modern Prometheus*, had been filmed three times in the silent era (once by Thomas Edison) before this talkie was produced. Not only was this Frankenstein the first to vocalize—actually he just grunted, cooed, and growled—but this was also the first version in any media in which Dr. Frankenstein mistakenly implanted the brain of a criminal into his creation. Boris Karloff went from a working actor to a star overnight with his surprisingly touching portrayal of the man-made monster. Through his ability to maintain an almost sensual innocence at all times, Karloff managed to embody both heroism and villainy in one character.

Visually, the monster comes on strong; according to makeup artist Jack Pierce, those were not bolts coming out of Karloff's neck but rather electric plugs, because "the monster was an electrical gadget and lightning was his life force."

(OPPOSITE) *The man-made monster in* Frankenstein *(Boris Karloff) is at once innocent and destructive.*

In depicting the monster as appealing, vulnerable, and very human, this *Frankenstein* effectively opened up the genre, making humane horror a cinematic possibility. The film has been endlessly remade, reworked, butchered, and bastardized. Among the more notable sequels are *Bride of Frankenstein* (1935); *Son of Frankenstein* (1939); *The Ghost of Frankenstein* (1942); *Frankenstein Meets the Wolfman* (1943); *House of Frankenstein* (1944); and *Abbott and Costello Meet Frankenstein* (1948).

Frankenstein (1931)   Boris Karloff, Colin Clive, Mae Clarke, Dwight Frye, John Boles, Edward van Sloan, Frederick Kerr, Lionel Belmore, and Michael Mark; directed by James Whale; screenplay by John L. Balderston, Garrett Fort, Francis Edward Faragoh, and Robert Florey (uncredited), based on the stage play by Peggy Webling, adapted from the novel by Mary Shelley; produced by Carl Laemmle, Jr.; Universal; 71 min. (b&w)

(PREVIOUS PAGES) *Klaus Kinski is Orlock, the vampire, in Werner Herzog's eerie, hypnotic remake of* Nosferatu *(see p. 27).*

A young beauty in The Howling *becomes fair game for evil creatures inhabiting a mountainside spa.*

The Howling

John Sayles's tongue-in-cheek screenplay opens with a familiar brand of horror, as a Los Angeles TV anchorwoman (Dee Wallace) goes undercover at a porn parlor in order to trap a maniac. In the aftermath of this traumatic experience, she goes to a nearby spa run by Patrick Macnee. Kindly Mr. Macnee isn't so kindly, however. He is the head of a cult of werewolves. In contrast to the usual film depictions of monsters as loners, these hirsuit guys and gals live together as a community with their own norms and values. Of course, if one is "invited" to join the pack, one joins . . . whether one wants to or not. That's what happens to Wallace. But dedicated reporter that she is, she delivers the exposé of her life—literally—when she transforms herself into a werewolf on the air in order to convince viewers of the danger in their midst.

In the film's most startling moment, Christopher Stone turns from man to werewolf convincingly, his temples throbbing, his jaw elongating, his hair and nails lengthening. But, overall, the film's campy quality too often distances viewers from the story's horrific possibilities. It is the genre's first glimpse of mating werewolves, and that's a howl. If they would have just given those guys a little more . . . respect. As it is, the scariest moment is the visually vivid transformation scene, and that comes halfway into the film.

The Howling (1981) Dee Wallace, Patrick Macnee, Dennis Dugan, Belinda Balaski, Christopher Stone, John Carradine, Dick Miller, Slim Pickens, Kevin McCarthy, and Elisabeth Brooks; directed by Joe Dante; screenplay by John Sayles; produced by Michael Fennell and Jack Conrade; Avco Embassy; 91 min. (c)

(OPPOSITE) *Superb special effects and makeup make the transformations in* The Howling *horrifyingly lifelike.*

Zombies rampage suburbia in George Romero's cult quickie, Night of the Living Dead.

Night of the Living Dead

A rocket launch goes awry and radiation from its satellite falls to earth. In director George Romero's ghoulish 1968 cult classic, the radiation awakens the dead, causing them to feed on the living. In Romero's world, nothing is certain, no logic is assured, no justice is hoped for. Family bonds are destroyed, as a teenage zombie attempts to kill his loving sister and a little living/dead girl munches on her adoring father, eating him organ by organ. Stunned by all that she sees going on around her, the film's heroine (Judith O'Dea) becomes near-catatonic and stays that way for the remainder of the film. Sounding an even more cynical note, the climax includes the gunning down of the hero (Duane Jones), who is mistaken for one of the walking dead.

Displaying a strong sense of pace, the director escalates the tension, as the film progresses and the zombies increase in number. This is powerfully dark material, shot on a shoestring over a couple of weekends in Pittsburgh. Though the acting and production values are often amateurish, the movie's impact cannot be denied.

Night of the Living Dead (1968)   Duane Jones, Russell Streiner, Judith O'Dea, Keith Wayne, Julia Ridley, Karl Hardman, and Marilyn Estman; directed by George Romero; screenplay by John Russo; produced by Russell Streiner and Karl Hardman; Image Ten; 96 min. (b&w)

I Was a Teenage Werewolf

With a teenage Michael Landon in the starring role, the film follows a misunderstood boy sent to a psychiatrist because he has some primal urges, among them a fondness for raw meat and a tendency toward enraged fits. The shrink, however, is something of a wacko himself, believing that mankind can only be saved from atomic annihilation by a return to primitive culture. To demonstrate his belief, the psychiatrist injects Landon with a magical serum, hypnotizes him, stands back, and watches. Still in his school letter jacket, Landon is transformed into a fanged werewolf, who then goes on the prowl, savagely butchering debs and grinds in between classes. Eventually, the teen werewolf kills the psychiatrist and then is killed himself by a cop.

The film has a distinct 1950s quality to it, sometimes resembling a social satire, often taking itself quite seriously. For some, this makes the movie very dated, even campy; for others, the 1950s atmosphere is just a better backdrop for horror. Pointed directly at the huge teenage market, the film cost a mere $150,000 to make, and it took in what was then a very hefty $2.5 million.

I Was a Teenage Werewolf (1957)   Michael Landon, Whit Bissell, Yvonne Lime, Tony Marshall, Dawn Richard, Barney Phillips, Ken Miller, and Eddie Mar; directed by Gene Fowler, Jr.; screenplay by Ralph Thornton; produced by Herman Cohen; Sunset Productions; 76 min. (b&w)

(OPPOSITE) *As the title character in* I Was a Teenage Werewolf, *Michael Landon gives new meaning to the term "making out."*

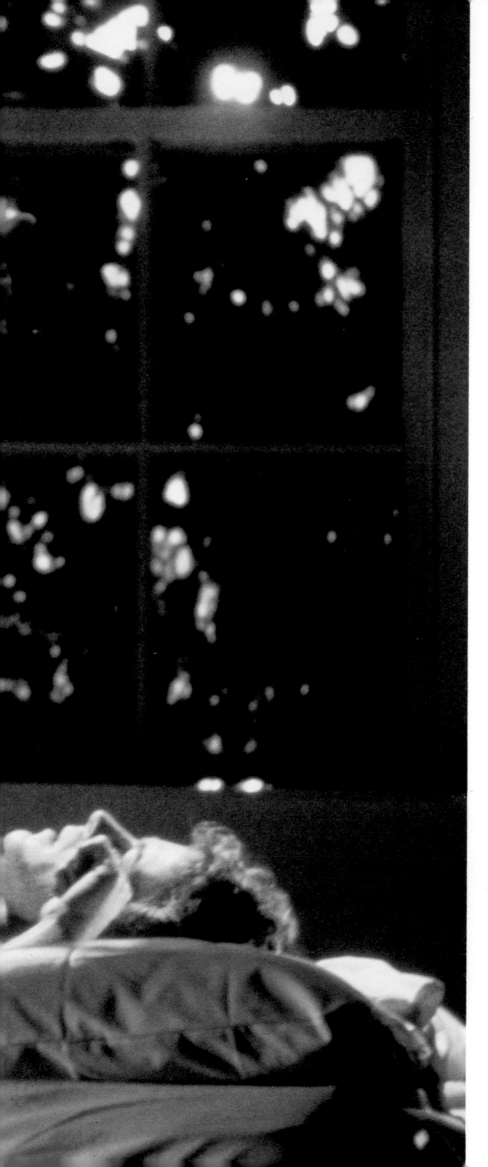

Cat People

According to producer Val Lewton, the formula for this film was simple: "A love story, three scenes of suggested horror and one of actual violence." Director Jacques Tourneur followed the formula, incorporating Fritz Lang's theory that nothing that can be shown is nearly as horrifying as that which the viewer can imagine. But the film is far more than formula, considerably more than theoretical.

Feline Simone Simon plays the lead, a Serbian-born fashion designer living in Manhattan. She falls in love and marries, but then fails to consummate the marriage out of a bizarre fear that she'll be transformed into a raging cat should her passions be aroused. Her feline traits are so subtly suggested—she paws the air near a canary cage and rakes her long fingernails across a couch—that vague, uneasy suspicions are gradually instilled in the viewer's mind. Because of her odd sexual aloofness, her husband takes a fancy to another woman, and from then on that other woman is stalked by an unseen, panther-like presence. When this rival walks through Central Park at night, paws can be heard padding through the darkness. Finally reaching the street, she is greeted by a screeching hiss … actually the opening doors of a bus. At the studio's insistence, the transformation is complete and shown at the film's conclusion; but embodied in a real panther, the cat lady ironically loses some of her force.

In a 1982 remake, director Paul Schrader features the striking Nastassia Kinski as his cat lady, a woman who can mate only with her similarly inflicted brother, played by Malcolm McDowell. Into this incestuous affair, he throws zookeeper John Heard, a man so smitten with the cat lady that he decides a night of love is worth the deathly outcome.

Cat People (1942) Simone Simon, Kent Smith, Tom Conway, Jane Randolph, Jack Holt, and Elizabeth Russell; directed by Jacques Tourneur; screenplay by DeWitt Bodeen; produced by Val Lewton; RKO; 74 min. (b&w)

"She knew strange, fierce pleasures that no other woman could ever feel," said the movie poster of Simone Simon, the troubled wife of Kent Smith, in Cat People.

In Paul Schrader's remake of Cat People *(1982), Nastassia Kinski turns into a black panther during a night of passion with zookeeper John Heard.*

As with Lugosi, Frank Langella first essayed the role of the vampire count on stage. He brought the same sensuous romanticism to the film version of Dracula *(1979).*

Dracula

"I am ... Dracula!" exclaims Bela Lugosi, and from that moment on everything he does and says is convincing. When offered a glass of wine, for example, he refuses, his eyes gleaming: "I never drink ... *wine*," he replies.

Starting off strongly, this prototype for all vampire films sets the stage with an atmospheric long shot of Dracula's somber castle in the Carpathian Mountains, emotionally underscoring the mood with a theme from Tchaikovsky's *Swan Lake*. Renfield (Dwight Frye) arrives at the castle to sell the Count some English real estate. Dracula takes one bite of this realtor, and Renfield is reduced to a primitive slave, subsisting on bugs and rodents.

Based largely on a Broadway play version of Bram Stoker's novel, the film turns unexpectedly talky and stiff when it takes the action to London. Scores of sequel *Dracula*'s have been shot, among them: *Dracula's Daughter* (1936) and *Son of Dracula* (1943). In a 1958 version, the towering Christopher Lee brings a real animal presence to the character, and with it, draws gobs of Technicolor blood, something quite new to the genre. And in a 1979 reworking, Frank Langella is a sensual, romantic Dracula in Edwardian England, a reign perhaps stronger in style than substance.

Dracula (1931) Bela Lugosi, Helen Chandler, Dwight Frye, David Manners, Edward van Sloan, Francis Dade, Herbert Bunston, and Moon Carroll; directed by Todd Browning; screenplay by Garret Fort and Dudley Murphy, based on the play by Hamilton Deane and John Balderston, adapted from the Bram Stoker novel; produced by Carl Laemmle, Jr.; Universal; 83 min. (b&w)

Bela Lugosi in the role he made famous, Dracula.

(OPPOSITE) *Hammer Studio's 1958 remake of* Dracula *starred Christopher Lee as the king of the undead.*

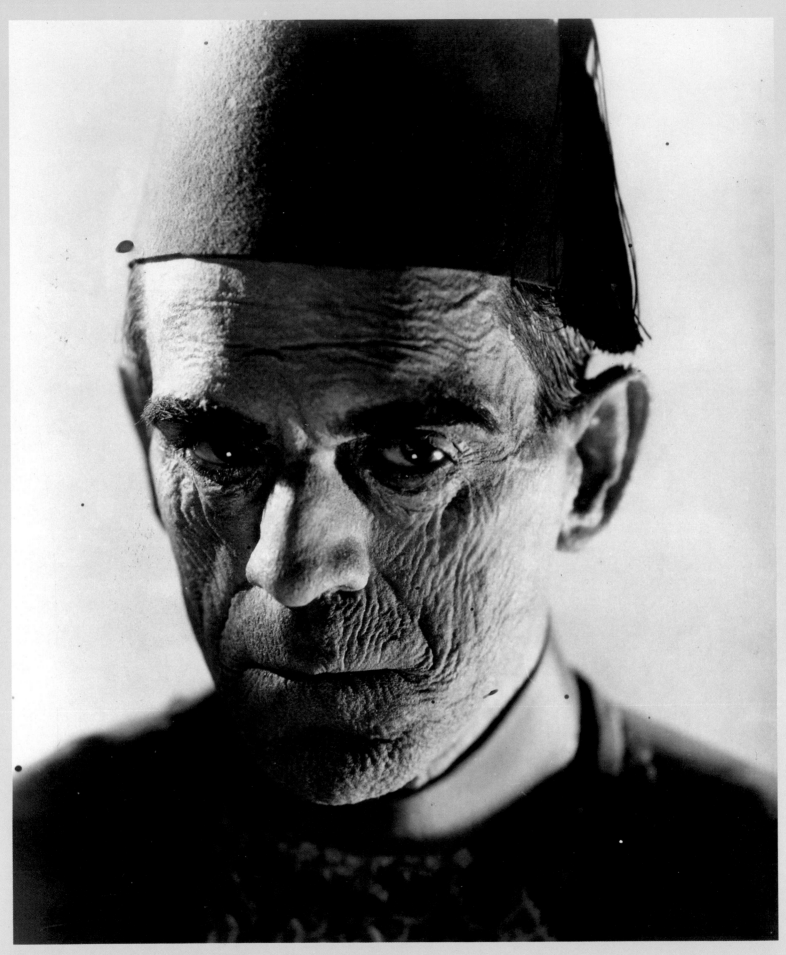

Boris Karloff is the parchment-skinned Ardath Bey, also known as The Mummy.

Archeologist Bramwell Fletcher mistakenly reads an ancient incantation that awakens the long-dead Im-ho-tep in The Mummy.

The Mummy

This was not the first *Mummy* on the block, but it is surely the best. It's Boris Karloff again, this time giving a dramatically different performance from that in *Frankenstein*, released the year before.

The story opens in Egypt, 1921. A team of British archeologists discovers the tomb of Im-ho-tep. Despite warnings of the dangers still lurking in the mausoleum, one young scientist stays behind when the group leaves. As the audience watches, he recites the ancient reincarnation prayer that brings the mummified Im-ho-tep (Karloff in a mud-and-glue-soaked cloth wrapping) to life behind him. Im-ho-tep escapes, while the young scientist, stunned and near hysterical, remains in the tomb. Cut to 1932. The Brits have returned to Egypt, and are met by an odd parchment-skinned man named Ardath Bey, actually the semisocialized Im-ho-tep. Bey is powerfully attracted to the half-Egyptian daughter of the British

Governor of Sudan (Zita Johann), and uncontrollably, she returns the fervor. Bey figures she is a reincarnation of Princess Anck-es-en-Amon, his lover 3700 years before. To ensure the immortality of her spirit, he decides to kill the girl, but he is interrupted by her fiancé (David Manners).

A rather trite and poorly executed flashback, seen in a magic pool, and an unsatisfying conclusion with Im-ho-tep disintegrating, disrupt an otherwise entertaining nightmare.

The Mummy (1932) Boris Karloff, Zita Johann, Edward van Sloan, David Manners, Arthur Byron, Bramwell Fletcher, Noble Johnson, Leonard Mudie, Eddie Kane, and Katherine Byron; directed by Karl Freund; screenplay by John L. Balderston; produced by Stanley Bergerman; Universal; 72 min. (b&w)

Scientist David Hedison tries to hide his shockingly altered appearance from his wife, Patricia Owens, in The Fly.

The Fly

In that paranoid decade, the 1950s, *The Fly* offered a refreshingly literate sci-fi saga that reinforced fears about scientists in pursuit of knowledge without regard for man's safety or survival.

This tale of a science experiment gone awry features a young scientist (David Hedison), who is working on a "matter transmitter" that can transform objects into energy, beam them through space, and reconstitute them at a distant receiver. When he tries to transmit himself across the lab, parts of Hedison get mixed up with parts of a fly which happens to be in the teleportation chamber. Rematerialized, the scientist finds he has the fly's head and arm and the fly has his facial features. Though the scientist/fly sometimes wears a black cloth over his head—possibly to ease the marital strain with his wife (Patricia Owens)—when he appears in all his disgusting glory, he's quite convincing. Similarly, the little fly with the little scientist's head is effective, especially when it cries out in a tiny voice: "Help me! Help me!" The two-part climax includes a scene in which the fly is trapped in a spider's web on the scientist's patio and one in which the scientist self-destructs in a hydraulic press, with assistance from his horrified wife.

Numerous sequels appeared, including *Return of the Fly* (1959) and *Curse of the Fly* (1963). And in 1986, director David Cronenberg remade the original, using the versatile Jeff Goldblum as the scientist, and Goldblum's real-life wife, Academy Award–winning Geena Davis, as the reporter with whom he gets romantically involved.

The Fly (1958)   David Hedison, Patricia Owens, Vincent Price, Herbert Marshall, Charles Herbert, and Kathleen Freeman; directed and produced by Kurt Neumann; screenplay by James Clavell; 20th Century Fox; 94 min. (c)

The 1986 remake of The Fly *finds Jeff Goldblum gradually transforming into a hideous insect-man.*

One of the screen's first horror classics, Nosferatu, *with Max Schreck as the vampire count, Orlock.*

The Wolf Man

"Even a man who is pure in heart, and says his prayers at night, may become a wolf when the wolfbane blooms, and the autumn moon is full and bright," warns the gypsy in *The Wolf Man*, and such is the fate of the young American, Larry Talbot (Lon Chaney, Jr.), who journeys to Wales to visit his ancestral home.

Enshrouded in a foggy, misty moor—like those so often seen in the genre—Talbot falls prey to a werewolf (Bela Lugosi) who changes his life forever. Puzzled by dreams in which he kills people, he turns to the gypsy for advice, and learns to his horror that he has been fanged by a werewolf and has indeed become a lycanthrope himself. Fearing the coming of the full moon, Talbot forcefully warns his fiancée to stay inside while he goes off to await the dreaded transformation. Hearing his emotional confession, she, of course, cannot stay housebound. At the climax, it is Talbot's father (Claude Rains) who stops the Wolf Man, clubbing his own son to death with a silver-handled cane.

Chaney's imaginative Wolf Man makeup was the work of Jack Pierce, who also created the Frankenstein monster and the Mummy for Boris Karloff. It took six hours to complete Chaney's transformation for each day's shooting, enabling the actor to say his lines from behind a rubber snout and a lot of yak hair.

The Wolf Man (1941)   Lon Chaney, Jr., Claude Rains, Evelyn Ankers, Bela Lugosi, Ralph Bellamy, Maria Ouspenskaya, Warren William, Patrick Knowles, and Fay Helm; directed and produced by George Waggner; screenplay by Curt Siodmak; Universal; 71 min. (b&w)

(OPPOSITE) The Wolf Man, *played by Lon Chaney, Jr., prepares to pounce on the unsuspecting Evelyn Ankers.*

Nosferatu

This superb, incredibly atmospheric German version of the Bram Stoker novel *Dracula* won acclaim from the European Surrealists before it had to be withdrawn from distribution because it infringed on the novel's copyright. Max Schreck, as the vampire Orlock, imbues his rat-like countenance with a powerful, creepy quality. At the film's fulcrum, however, is the virginal Nina (Greta Schroeder), who in this version does not need to be rescued from the clutches of the vampire because she wishes to obliterate his evil. The movie's climax shows the sexual-spiritual fusion of these two, with Nina undergoing the dramatic change, transformed by the power of her new sexual knowledge. As the sun rises, she is no longer the same woman and, having lost all her innocence, she dies.

Director F. W. Murnau and screenwriter Henrik Galeen departed from Stoker's standard vampire myth by sending Nosferatu on a sea journey, by making him cast a shadow, and by making sunlight fatal to him. Though sometimes slow going, every frame of the film powerfully contributes to the chilling mood. Some scenes strike the viewer as impressionistic, others surrealistic, and rarely has light been so subtly captured on film. A milestone in the genre, Murnau's *Nosferatu* influenced everything from subsequent vampire films to Jean Cocteau's remarkable *Beauty and the Beast* (1946).

In a 1979 remake, the accomplished Werner Herzog tackled the theme in *Nosferatu the Vampyre*, with the dynamic Klaus Kinski as Orlock. Eerie and hypnotic in its own way, this color remake shows a sleazier vampire, but one no less fascinating to watch.

Nosferatu (1922)   Max Schreck, Alexander Granach, Gustav von Wangenheim, Greta Schroeder, G. H. Schnell, and Ruth Landshoff; directed by F. W. Murnau; screenplay by Henrik Galeen; Prana Films; 95 min.; silent (b&w)

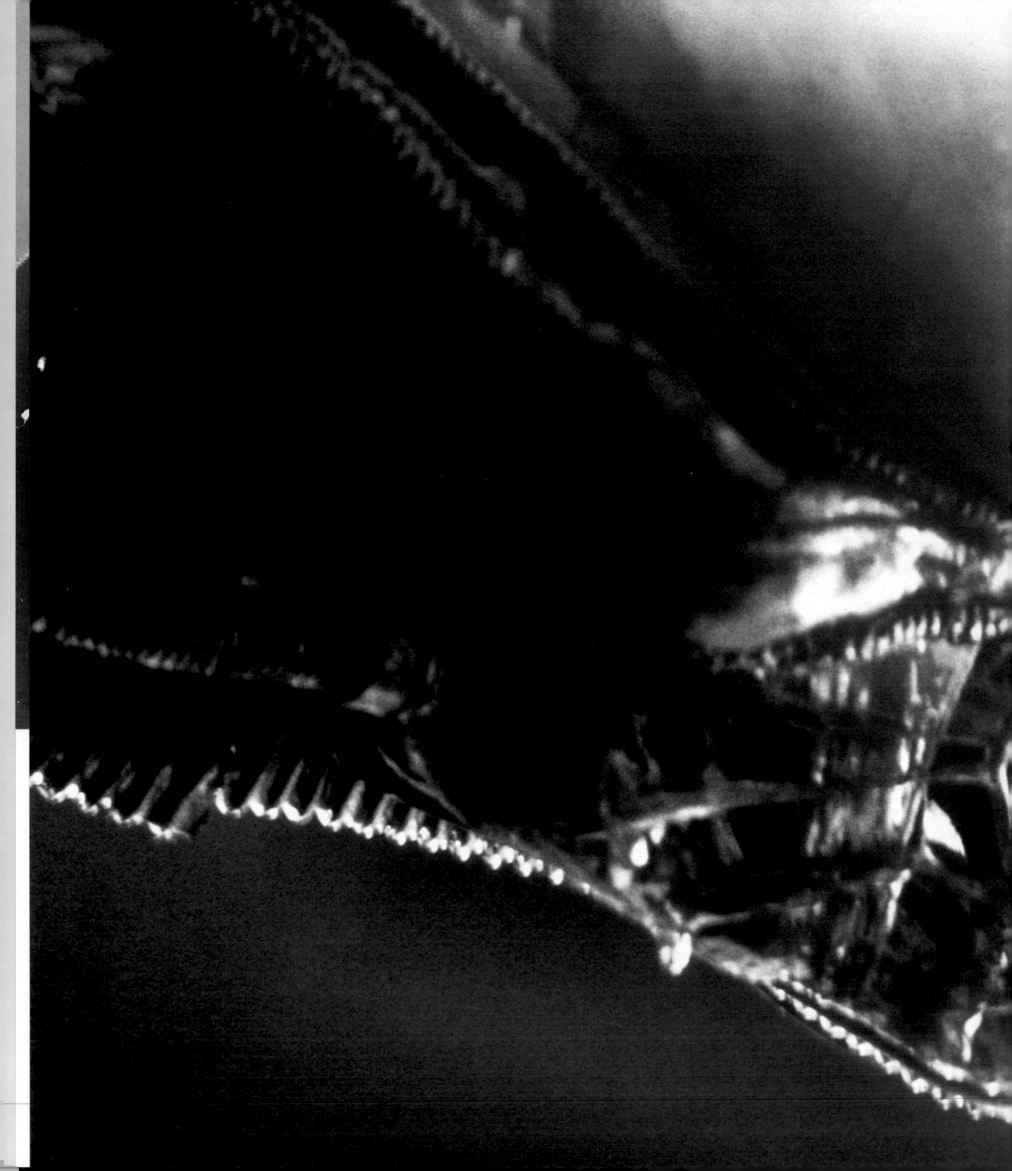

ALIENS

A team of scientists and soldiers led by Kenneth Tobey (center) discovers that The Thing, *an alien creature frozen in the arctic ice, has escaped.*

The Thing

A breakthrough in postwar horror, this film probed for fears deeper than those inspired by the threat of nuclear destruction, and found them … in aliens from outer space. Indeed, its quasi-scientific tone is the perfect foil for science fiction mayhem.

At an army research station in the Arctic, a strange, unidentified object is found buried in the ice. The researchers fan out to trace the outline of the object, and discover that they're standing over an enormous flying saucer. Eventually, they get to meet the spaceship's captain, a swell-headed "vegoid" played by James Arness. Although the vegoid's claws are menacing, one of his arms is easily chewed off "just like a carrot" by a dog. But the vegoid is completely capable of regenerating limbs and makes himself whole again. Furthermore, he's capable of reproducing himself, by dropping seeds into soil fertilized by human blood. Since human blood is in short supply up at this remote Arctic outpost, the creature must tap into the source closest to hand. To his relief, vegoid Arness finds there's really plenty of local fertilizer for an alien victory garden. Eventually though, he's caught in a trap, stunned by an electric arc which cooks him well done.

A 1982 remake by John Carpenter had incredible visuals, which unfortunately overwhelmed the material. In Carpenter's version, the vegoid is closer to the protoplasmic creature described in the John Campbell novella on which both films are based. But the special effects in the remake are rarely the result of plot development, so they unintentionally pull the audience away from the story.

The Thing (1951) Kenneth Tobey, Margaret Sheridan, Robert Cornthwaite, Dewey Martin, James Arness, and William Self; directed by Christian Nyby; screenplay by Charles Lederer, based on the novella by John Campbell; produced by Howard Hawks; RKO; 87 min. (b&w)

In John Carpenter's 1982 remake of The Thing, *the shape-changing creature displays a bizarre imagination.*

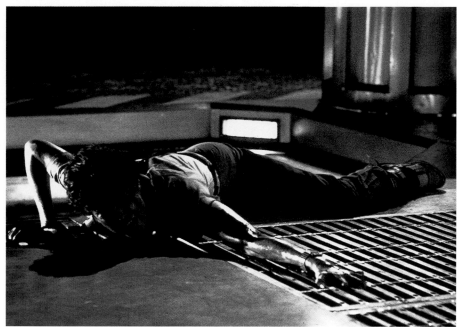

Aliens *(1986) finds Sigourney Weaver hanging on for dear life in her war against the race of creatures that destroyed her crew in the film's predecessor.*

Alien

A nightmarish visual feast, *Alien* stands as perhaps the most graphically successful blending of sci-fi and horror to date. Fantastic "biomechanical" sets resembling human body parts—the work of Swiss artist, H. R. Giger—provide an eerie backdrop for terror in outer space. And the monster, from the hand of E.T.-creator Carlo Rambaldi, is thoroughly frightening and repulsive in its several guises on the path toward adult maturity. Director Ridley Scott infuses fresh life into the storyline of a group of people being killed off one by one, creating in the process, a film of notable vitality.

The film opens as a corporate-owned space tanker is returning from deep space when it stops on an uncharted planet to answer a distress call. The planet is covered with pods, and from one, a yellow crab-like creature springs onto astronaut John Hurt's helmet. Brought into the spacecraft, the creature eventually dies, but not before laying its eggs in Hurt's body. A baby creature's escape from its unwilling host is truly horrifying, and from then on, the audience sits tight and prays, as Sigourney Weaver leads the crew on a terrifying fight to find the creature that is preying upon them.

In the 1986 sequel, *Aliens,* hard-hitting director James Cameron has Weaver return for revenge against the race of creatures, and get it. The new monsters look like they were rescued from the backlot of a 1950s Japanese sci-fi maker, but Sigourney gets to sit in and operate a 25-foot-tall industrial robot, and that's a sight worth the price of admission.

Alien (1979) Tom Skerritt, Sigourney Weaver, Veronica Cartwright, Harry Dean Stanton, John Hurt, Ian Holm, and Yaphet Kotto; directed by Ridley Scott; screenplay by Dan O'Bannon; produced by Gordon Carroll and David Giler; 20th Century Fox; 124 min. (c)

The horrific creature in Alien *stalks the crew of a space tanker answering a distress signal on a remote planet.*

Steve McQueen (in his first screen role) and Aneta Corseaut save their town from the ravages of The Blob.

The Blob

A meteor flames to earth, and from it a blob-like mass of primordial goo emerges. Soon, the blob is enveloping and sucking up people, growing ever more massive with each individual. The blob oozes around town, feeding in a supermarket, then moving on to the movies, where it engulfs the projectionist before sliding down to devour the audience.

In his first cinematic role, Steve McQueen steps to the fore as one tough character, a man clearly able to stand up to amorphous aliens. McQueen and Aneta Corseaut catch sight of the blob, observing it devour the town's doctor and his nurse. But when they report it, no one believes them. Similarly, when a group of teenage hotrodders spot the blob and report it to the police, they're dismissed as pranksters. It is these renegade teenagers, though, who save the town, discovering that the blob hates the cold. In a matter of movie minutes, the blob is stunned, stuffed into an air transport, and flown to the Antarctic, where it is dropped to its death.

The movie's title track, "The Blob," was as successful as the film, proving to be the first and only major hit for the Five Blobs. In a 1988 remake of the film, director Chuck Russell puts a new, state-of-the-art blob through its paces, serving up something scarier than the original.

The Blob (1958)   Steve McQueen, Aneta Corseaut, Earl Rowe, and Olin Howlin; directed by Irvin S. Yeaworth, Jr.; screenplay by Theodore Simonson and Kate Phillips; produced by Jack H. Harris; Paramount; 85 min. (c)

(OPPOSITE) *In the 1988 remake of* The Blob, *the shapeless ectoplasmic predator turns up in the most unlikely places.*

The mad sculptor played by Vincent Price is in hot pursuit of his next "lifelike" wax statue in House of Wax.

House of Wax

This remake of Warner's 1933 *Mystery of the Wax Museum* tells the story of a wax museum owner (Vincent Price), literally defaced by a horrible accident, who turns to murder in order to bolster his collection of sculpted people. Thus, instead of creating the life-size figures from scratch, he dips his murder victims into wax, turning them into remarkably realistic evocations of Joan of Arc, Edwin Booth, and other famous folk. With a pair of detectives closing in on him, he attempts to "immortalize" the suspicious friend of one of his victims—the film's heroine Phyllis Kirk—but he falls into a vat of boiling wax himself, a fitting demise for this demonic sculptor.

In telling this grisly story, the film was a pioneer in the use of 3-D. At the time that it was made, studios, faced with increasing competition from that emerging medium, TV, were eager to give their viewers experiences unavailable at home. Screens got larger. Stereophonic sound was introduced. Gimmicks that aroused other senses—smell, touch—were also tried. Often the results were unsuccessful dramatically but here, in large part, they work, thanks to director André de Toth, a firm believer in the horrific possibilities of 3-D. (Ironically de Toth was blind in one eye and couldn't actually appreciate the effects of 3-D himself.) Few scenes are wasted on mere effect, however. Most of them skillfully combine real drama with jump-of-the-screen action.

House of Wax (1953)   Vincent Price, Frank Lovejoy, Phyllis Kirk, Carolyn Jones, Paul Picerni, Roy Roberts, and Charles Buchinsky (Charles Bronson); directed by André de Toth; screenplay by Crane Wilbur, based on a story by Charles Beiden; produced by Bryan Foy; Warner Brothers; 88 min.; 3-D (c)

When his unscrupulous partner sets fire to his wax musuem in House of Wax, *Vincent Price is caught in the blaze and becomes horribly disfigured.*

(PREVIOUS PAGES) *Jason, the demonic hockey-masked killer, has slashed his way through seven* Friday the 13th *movies. This is from the first (see pp. 68-69)*

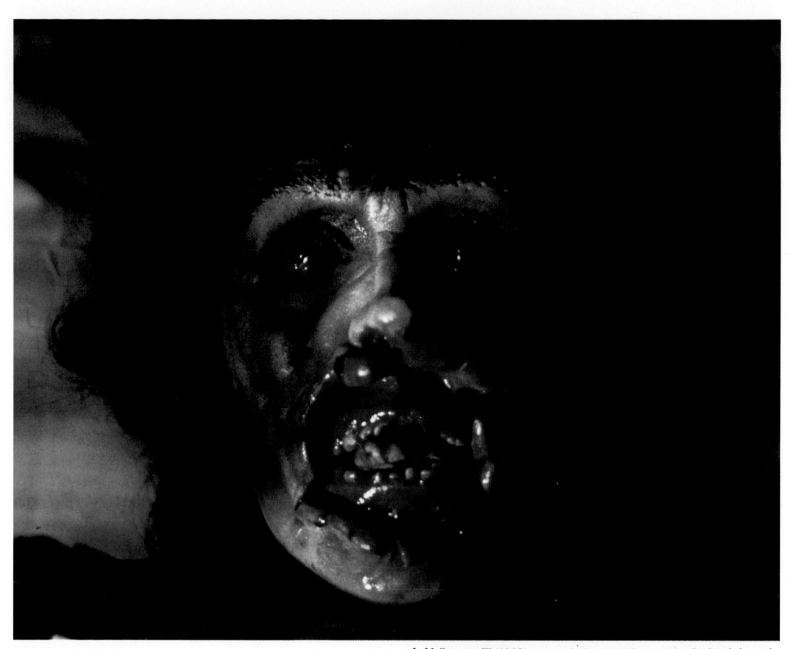

In Halloween III *(1983) a new plot line, revolving around a fiendish mask-maker, is introduced.*

Halloween

An insubstantial story turns into dynamite in the hands of horror specialist John Carpenter, who stretches the Panavision frame to include what's lurking just beyond, toying with audience expectations, fooling with their fears. In the opening sequence, for example, viewers see someone watching through a window, staring at a teenage couple necking. The "someone" is then in the house, suddenly in the kitchen, selecting a butcher knife. The person then commits a bloody murder, and—as if in horror—the camera pulls back to show the killer is a six-year-old boy.

Fifteen years later, the boy, Michael Myers, escapes from an asylum and returns home to exorcise more demons, as he had exorcised his sister (the girl necking). Back in his old neighborhood, three teenage cuties spark distant memories and, one by one, he hunts them down on Halloween night, despite the best efforts of the psychiatrist (Donald Pleasence) who treated him and is now stalking him.

What makes this nightmare stand out is not the story but the telling, the almost perverse trickery of John Carpenter's direction. The narrative gets viewers tense, relaxes them, then stabs them in the throat.

The 1981 *Halloween II* picked up where the original left off, with much of the action taking place in the hospital where Jamie Lee Curtis, one of Michael's victims in the first film, is attempting her recovery. By *Halloween III* (1983), a whole new story about a fiendish Halloween maskmaker was introduced.

Halloween (1978)   Donald Pleasence, Jamie Lee Curtis, Nancy Loomis, P. J. Soles, Charles Cyphers, Kyle Richards, Tony Moran, and Will Sandin; directed by John Carpenter; screenplay by John Carpenter and Debra Hill; produced by Debra Hill; Universal; 91 min. (c)

(OPPOSITE) *Laurie Strode (Jamie Lee Curtis) seeks refuge from the manic Michael Myers in* Halloween II *(1981).*

Glenn Close simply won't be denied in Fatal Attraction, *no matter what Michael Douglas does.*

Fatal Attraction

In 1987, everyone was talking about *Fatal Attraction* because it served up a nightmare that could happen to virtually anyone. After all, most of us have been momentarily attracted to a stranger. One-night stands—even among married people—are not exactly uncommon. But few people expect to be bound forever to the object of momentary passion; or to risk death as a result of a chance encounter. Yet, in this film, that's exactly what happens to attorney Michael Douglas, who has what he presumes to be a little fling while the wife (Anne Archer) is away, only to find that his sex partner (Glenn Close) thinks it must last forever. Close is dogged and will not be denied, even if it means killing herself or Douglas.

Tightly scripted and directed, the film delivers several fine performances, especially from Close, who manages to create a person who is instantly likable. Her rapport with the audience, like her rapport with Douglas, is immediate. When she turns on her lover and becomes malicious, she still manages to retain some level of audience sympathy. After all, she's fighting for her notion of love.

Eventually though, most viewers' feelings swing to Douglas and Archer, who are trying to protect their family from an invader.

The original ending had Close kill herself, but test audiences found it unsatisfying. So director Adrian Lyne opted for a resolution that requires both husband and wife to kill her. That Close possesses an awesome strength or will to live which renders her incredibly difficult to kill is perhaps her strongest link to the maniacs of the slasher films, notably Jason of the *Friday the 13th* series and Michael Myers of *Halloween. Fatal Attraction* is a modern nightmare with universal appeal, and it marked a stunning step forward for the genre.

Fatal Attraction (1987) Michael Douglas, Glenn Close, Anne Archer, Ellen Foley, and Stuart Pankin; directed by Adrian Lyne; screenplay by James Dearden; produced by Stanley Jaffe and Sherry Lansing; Paramount; 120 min. (c)

(OPPOSITE) *Obsessive love has reduced capable career woman Alex Forrest (Glenn Close) to a deeply depressed state in* Fatal Attraction.

A Nightmare on Elm Street

"T wilight Zone" had taken the audience there before, to that place where dreams affect reality, and to the place beyond, where dreams *become* reality. In *A Nightmare on Elm Street*, director/screenwriter Wes Craven brings that place to suburban Los Angeles as he follows a group of teens who inexplicably begin to meet the same madman—Freddy Krueger (Robert Englund)—in their dreams. Eventually, most of them end up horribly murdered, mutilated by the dream man with the razor-tipped fingers.

Craven has crafted some powerful imagery here, tapping into both the mood and tone of a horrifying nightmare while playing with the intriguing question of what is real, what is fantasy, and how the two intermesh. Special effects are special indeed, most notably the one in which a bed swallows up a sleeping teen, then spouts a geyser of blood. Unfortunately, as the film moves toward its conclusion, it becomes more fragmented rather than more focused. Maybe it was *all* a dream, the film suddenly suggests, or maybe not.

Any way it's interpreted, one thing is clear—horror fans loved *A Nightmare on Elm Street*, so much so that it spawned three sequels: *A Nightmare on Elm Street 2: Freddy's Revenge* (1986), in which the razor-tipped Freddy Krueger got top billing; *A Nightmare on Elm Street 3: Dream Warriors* (1987), in which Freddy got to slash those fingertips some more; and *A Nightmare on Elm Street 4: The Dream Master* (1988), in which Freddy killed off the survivors from *Elm Street 3*. There are some good moments in all three of these sequels, though *Elm Street 2* tends toward the camp at times.

A Nightmare on Elm Street (1984)   John Saxon, Ronee Blakley, Heather Langenkamp, Amanda Weiss, Nick Corri, Johnny Depp, and Robert Englund; directed and written by Wes Craven; produced by Robert Shaye; New Line Cinema/Media Home Entertainment/Smart Egg Pictures; 91 min. (c)

(FAR RIGHT) *The telephone comes to life in Heather Langenkamp's hand, a sampling of the bizarre and frightening imagery in* A Nightmare on Elm Street.

(RIGHT) *Freddy seeks to end the life of Tuesday Night, one of the few Elm Street survivors, in* A Nightmare on Elm Street 4: The Dream Master *(1988).*

(BELOW) *In snake-like fashion, Freddy Kruger (Robert Englund) attempts to devour one of his teen victims in* A Nightmare on Elm Street 3: Dream Warriors *(1987).*

Leatherface enjoys a moment of sheer ecstacy in Tobe Hooper's grisly slasher film, The Texas Chainsaw Massacre.

The Texas Chainsaw Massacre

This early, low-budget slasher film is about as gruesome as they get. Like the much milder *Psycho*, it was based on the evil doings of Ed Gein, the Wisconsin fellow who liked to cut people up and make things out of their skin.

In this one, a group of kids visits the old family home in backwoods Texas. Surrounded by junk cars, the house is now occupied by inbred cannibals. Grandpa heads the clan of flesh eaters, boasting of his killing spree. But his real pride and joy is Leatherface, a squealing madman who wears a mask made from a human face and who totes around … a McCulloh chainsaw. The kids and the cannibals clash, and it isn't the kids who come out on top. One of them (Marilyn Burns), gets the worst of it, as she is hung on a meat hook and forced to watch her boyfriend get sliced into steaks.

Cinematically, the film is almost as strong as the subject matter, relentlessly forcing the viewer to watch the grisly action. It shows lots of it, but not everything. Even after all the slasher films that have followed in its wake, this movie remains one of the most horrifying visions ever put on film.

The Texas Chainsaw Massacre (1974) Marilyn Burns, Allen Danziger, Paul A. Partain, William Vail, Teri McMinn, Edwin Neal, Jim Siedow, Gunnar Hansen, and John Dugan; directed and produced by Tobe Hooper; screenplay by Kim Henkel and Tobe Hooper; Vortex; 81 min. (c)

Angie Dickinson is murdered in an elevator by a knife-wielding maniac in Dressed to Kill.

Dressed to Kill

Director Brian De Palma's slightly awkward homage to Alfred Hitchcock is loosely modeled on *Psycho*. Indeed, the film has not one but two shower scenes, either of which could end in murder but *neither* of which does. Rather, these episodes represent the sexual fantasies of a bored, upper-middle-class Manhattanite played by Angie Dickinson. The fantasies turn real, however, when she picks up a one-night stand in a museum. But it isn't her lover who kills her; it is a slasher who brutally takes her life in an elevator after her tryst. As with *Psycho*, the movie isn't over when the heroine is dead for, as with *Psycho*, a new protagonist, in the form of the victim's sibling, takes her place. In this case, that is Dickinson's brother (Keith Gordon), whose search for his sister's killer—with the assistance of a prostitute played by De Palma favorite Nancy Allen—leads him to Dickinson's shrink (Michael Caine). Like Anthony Perkins in *Psycho*, he is gentle and understanding until he dons women's clothes to kill those who arouse his hated masculine side

—hence, the movie's title. A coda, similar to that used by the director in *Carrie*, finds Caine escaping from the mental institution to which he has been committed and going after Allen. But, as in its telekinetic predecessor, it's a dream.

Angie Dickinson is fine as the bored housewife, but Michael Caine seems rather miscast as the transvestite psychiatrist. Thus, when his evil secret is revealed, what should be startling is instead rather unbelievable. Despite the disappointing climax, De Palma has crafted a film filled with tension and dread. Some of the suspense is manipulative, however, as scenes build to their nail-biting conclusions, only to emerge as dreams or fantasies.

Dressed to Kill (1980)   Michael Caine, Angie Dickinson, Nancy Allen, Keith Gordon, and Dennis Franz; directed and written by Brian De Palma; produced by George Litto; Cinema 77/Filmways/Warwick Associates; 104 min. (c)

Friday the 13th Part III *(1982) offers this particularly grisly moment in filmmaking. In 3-D, no less.*

Friday the 13th

After Universal's huge success with *Halloween*, other studios cast about for projects to cash in on the obvious appeal of blood and gore. Paramount, in particular, went to work on a teen movie that could match it for murderous mayhem. The result was *Friday the 13th*, the story of ill-fated Camp Crystal, a locale for murder some 20 years before.

As the film opens, half a dozen teen counselors are settling into the newly reopened camp. Then Jason shows up. A skulking force in a hockey mask, Jason wastes little time in eliminating just about every counselor at camp. Jason hacks, chops, and even drills the teenagers to death. With just one woman left at camp (Adrienne King), the friendly neighbor lady (Betsy Palmer) reveals that it is she who is Jason, she who is killing counselors in revenge for the death of her son, drowned at the camp some 20 years earlier. A fight ensues, a fight to the death, and though King wins, it may be a hollow victory. For as the movie ends, audiences are left with the possibility that Jason might still be out there.

Six sequels have been filmed, among them: *Friday the 13th Part II* (1981); *Friday the 13th Part III*, in 3-D (1982); *Friday the 13th—the Final Chapter* (1984); *Friday the 13th—A New Beginning* (1985); and *Friday the 13th Part VII—The New Blood* (1988). This is a bad dream that seems to go on forever.

Friday the 13th (1980)   Betsy Palmer, Adrienne King, Jeannine Taylor, Robbi Morgan, Kevin Bacon, Harry Crosby, Laurie Bartram, Mark Nelson, Peter Brouwer, and Walt Gorney; directed and produced by Sean S. Cunningham; screenplay by Victor Miller; Georgetown/Paramount; 95 min. (c)

(OPPOSITE) *By* Friday the 13th Part VII *(1988), the unstoppable Jason had graduated from teens to adults and to ever more inventive ways of dispensing his victims.*

CREATURES

Smitten by Julie Adams, the gill-man in The Creature from the Black Lagoon *follows her underwater, imitating her every move.*

Creature from the Black Lagoon

This classic 1950s creature feature finds a group of scientists paddling through the jungles of the Amazon in the hope of finding a creature that links man to his prehistoric roots. In a secluded lagoon, they find him in the form of a gill-man, a human-like lizard who studies them while they attempt to study him. He is particularly drawn to the female member of the expedition, Julie Adams, displaying an uncanny ability to imitate her when she swims. Eventually, he kidnaps her and, when her fiancé, Richard Denning, the bombastic leader of the expedition, fails to rise to the occasion, the insecure Richard Carlson, a fellow scientist who is also in love with Adams, follows the creature to his underwater lair and rescues the damsel in distress.

Originally released in 3-D, the film is at its best underwater, where it offers some truly spectacular sequences. Although it was shot on a low budget on the Universal Studio's jungle set, it still manages to convey the forbidding quality of Earth at its most primitive. As for the reptile-man, he is not evil. Rather, like Kong before him, he is simply misunderstood. Indeed, he has a strange kind of beauty, once you get to know him. Apparently 1950s audiences thought so. Despite his death at the end of the picture, he was revived for two sequels, *Revenge of the Creature* (1955), in which he is taken to Florida, and *The Creature Walks Among Us* (1956), in which he develops lungs and hits the streets.

Creature from the Black Lagoon (1954)   Richard Carlson, Julie Adams, Richard Denning, Antonio Moreno, Nestor Paiva, Ricou Browning, Ben Chapman, and Tom Hennessy; directed by Jack Arnold; screenplay by Harry Essex and Arthur Ross; produced by William Alland; Universal-International; 79 min. (b&w and on some prints, 3-D)

(OPPOSITE) *The* Creature from the Black Lagoon *terrifies Julie Adams, but the stalwart Richard Carlson stands ready to defend the woman he loves.*

At the climax of Them!, James Arness leads a team of soldiers to the lair of the incubating ants.

Them!

Director Gordon Douglas used a dry documentary approach to give extra impact to this sci-fi tale of ants, mutated into giants by atomic tests in the New Mexican desert. Much of this film's shock value lay in the recent discovery of atomic energy and the unpredictability of its potential. By merging science news with theoretically credible science fiction, *Them!* was frightening the way that TV news disasters are frightening: both prompt viewers to mutter under their breath, "There, but for the grace of God, go I."

Of course, if the ants had stayed in the desert, there wouldn't have been much of a story. But they swarm into the Los Angeles sewer system, finish off a freight car full of sugar, and kill whoever gets in their way with lethal injections of formic acid. These 15-foot-long monsters look mighty formidable here, and just about everybody runs for dear life. But when the creatures retreat into their hiding place, they leave a trail of sweet-smelling formic acid that tips off the army. Finally, the jumbo ants get cornered by James Arness and his fellow soldiers, who torch Them with flamethrowers. Them is fightin' words, apparently.

Them! (1954) James Whitmore, Edmund Gwenn, Joan Weldon, Onslow Stevens, James Arness, and Fess Parker; directed by Gordon Douglas; screenplay by David Sherdeman; produced by David Weisbart; Warner Brothers; 94 min. (b&w)

(OPPOSITE) *Giant ants strike terror in the heart of the New Mexican desert in* Them!

A horrible death comes to this skinny-dipping beauty in Jaws.

Jaws

What happens to a small New England resort community when it becomes the hunting ground for a great white shark? That is the question raised by this gripping movie, based on the best-selling novel by Peter Benchley. The answer is that some residents, like the town's mayor (Murray Hamilton) are willing to make their family and friends fishbait, if need be, to keep the tourists coming in. Others, like a wealthy shark expert (Richard Dreyfuss), want to capture the great white behemoth so they can study it. Still others, like the obsessed sea captain (Robert Shaw), want to kill it because it needs killing. At the center of these opposing forces is the town's police captain, Chief Brody (Roy Scheider), who simply wants to do his job. Director Steven Spielberg holds these disparate forces together in this, his second feature film, as he builds terror scene by scene out of a scenario that could happen at any summer resort community, reminding beach-goers in the process of just what might be lurking as they go in for a little dip. After all, this is no alien, no sci-fi monster. This merciless killer lurks near most beaches, sometimes way offshore, sometimes

Kids swimming in a lagoon scurry to elude the swiftly moving fin in Jaws. One can almost hear John Williams's pulsing music in the background.

quite close. Here then is a horror that *has* happened and *will* happen—to individuals and to communities.

The combination of Bob Mattey's mechanical shark, footage of actual great whites, Verna Fields's editing, John Williams's score, and Steven Spielberg's direction yields horrific action sequences of remarkable power. The seashore hasn't been the same since. Sequels included *Jaws 2* (1978) and *Jaws 3-D* (1983). But apparently the shark had only one good movie in him.

Jaws (1975) Roy Scheider, Robert Shaw, Richard Dreyfuss, Lorraine Gary, Murray Hamilton, Carl Gottlieb, and Peter Benchley; directed by Steven Spielberg; screenplay by Peter Benchley and Carl Gottlieb, from the novel by Peter Benchley; produced by Richard Zanuck and David Brown; Universal; 125 min. (c)

One of filmdom's favorite creatures is Godzilla, seen here enjoying a late afternoon snack.

Godzilla

In this Japanese answer to *King Kong*, a 250-foot-tall, 400-ton prehistoric monster who is revived by Pacific A-bomb tests, lays waste to Tokyo with a nastiness unparalleled in modern monsterdom. Where Kong could only tromp on things and crush stuff in his large hands, Godzilla can also flail his awesome tail and, most horrible of all, breathe on people with his radioactive breath. This deadly halitosis can be seen in the form of an atomic jetstream, and for both friends and enemies, it means that conversations with Godzilla are short. The military throws everything they've got at the monster, but it seems that only a power equal to Godzilla's can possibly stop him. That means trotting out the secret "oxygen destroyer," a bit of armament so potent that its inventor commits hara-kiri rather than reveal it.

Something of a camp folk hero in Japan, Godzilla enjoyed a 30-year career, during which he starred in 16 films. In this initial installment, as in the rest of those filmed before 1972, the monster was portrayed by actor Haruo Nakajima in a 100-pound Godzilla suit. And in 1962's *King Kong vs. Godzilla*, the two mega-monsters slugged it out atop Mt. Fuji.

Godzilla (1954) Raymond Burr, Takashi Shimura, Momoko Kochi, Akira Takarada, Akihiko Hirata, and Sachio Sakai; directed by Terry Morse and Inoshiro Honda; screenplay by Takeo Murata and Inoshiro Honda, from a story by Shigeru Kayama; produced by Tomoyuki Tanaka; Toho; 80 min. (b&w)

Willard

Rats again! When mama's boy Willard (Bruce Davison) is told by his domineering mother (Elsa Lanchester) to rid their creepy old mansion of its rats, the young man takes a liking to the creatures and soon has them doing his evil bidding. After he uses them to commit a robbery, he turns their malevolence against his mean boss (Ernest Borgnine), who he believes was instrumental in his father's death.

Though the film initially offers echoes of Hitchcock's *Psycho* (1960), it begins to go astray when the hammy little devils start overacting. It's not their fault, really, but after their first killing, director Daniel Mann seems to succumb to their furry cuteness, and the sense of horror is all but forgotten. Davison, however, maintains his own, and his transition from put-upon son to vengeful killer holds the film together.

Adapting his own novel, screenwriter Gilbert Ralston saw the movie as "a rat morality play." Consequently, much of the plot is an elaborate excuse for examining the psychological motivations of the story's principal characters. Director Mann's cheap stock shot of the rats supposedly devouring Borgnine further undercuts the horror. Nevertheless, the film was a success at the box office, and spawned a sequel, *Ben* (1972), which picked up right where the rats left off.

Willard (1970) Bruce Davison, Ernest Borgnine, Elsa Lanchester, Sondra Locke, Michael Dante, and J. Pat O'Malley; directed by Daniel Mann; screenplay by Gilbert A. Ralston, from his novel; produced by Mort Briskin; Cinerama/Bing Crosby; 95 min. (c)

A strange young man (Bruce Davison) sics his pet rats on his malevolent employer (Ernest Borgnine) in Willard.

Tippi Hedren is driven to a near catatonic state when she is trapped in a small room filled with flying feathered creatures in The Birds.

The Birds

There isn't a complicated plot here: man's fine feathered friends suddenly and inexplicably start attacking humankind, in a series of random, unprovoked battles. But it's not the storyline that holds this Hitchcock classic together, it's the interplay of haunting images, depicting our usually benign "feathered friends" turned horribly malignant. The Evan Hunter script (from a Daphne du Maurier novel) never unravels the mystery of this avian turnabout, but in this movie the lack of a cogent explanation merely adds to the feeling that nature is out of balance.

The story begins when bored playgirl Melanie Daniels (Tippi Hedren) impulsively buys a pair of lovebirds in a San Francisco pet store. She tries to deliver them to the attractive attorney she's just met (Rod Taylor), but he has gone off to the small coastal town of Bodega Bay to be with his family and she decides to follow. There, she is attacked by a group of birds. It puts her into shock, but those around her are sure it was a freak accident. Soon, however, the birds begin attacking everybody. And the war is on. Where it will end—and how—no one knows, for the movie ends as the terror seems about to spread inland.

Set primarily in Bodega Bay, the environment seems always to suggest the infinite—the ocean, the sky. But with the beauty of nature, the storyteller seems to say, man must also take its unpredictable terror.

The Birds (1963) Rod Taylor, Tippi Hedren, Jessica Tandy, Suzanne Pleshette, and Ethel Griffies; directed and produced by Alfred Hitchcock; screenplay by Evan Hunter, from the novel by Daphne du Maurier; Universal; 119 min. (c)

(OPPOSITE) *Rod Taylor is shocked when a tiny crow goes on the attack in* The Birds.

The enormity of the hairy mutant spider in Tarantula *becomes apparent when his pincers descend into an ordinary living room. The woman of the house doesn't look prepared for unexpected guests.*

Tarantula

In the post-Hiroshima era of the 1950s, there was increasing conflict between interest groups pushing the progress of science and those trying to maintain the balance of nature. What better way to illustrate that growing rift, the execs at Twentieth Century Fox must have thought, than a film about a furry little spider which gets a dose of a new growth hormone and grows to enormous size. "Giant spider strikes!" proclaimed the movie's poster; "... crawling terror 100 feet high!" Like other gargantuan beasts before it, this creepy eight-legged critter is depicted towering over the city, a beautiful woman in its grasp. But this one has a big advantage over its predecessors in that spiders already terrify most of us.

The story follows the doings of an elderly, already-deformed scientist hard at work in the Arizona desert. When he mistakenly splashes an experimental growth hormone on a spider, all hell is let loose, with the spider quickly growing to thousands of times its normal size. The tarantula runs amok, terrorizing the townsfolk before the U.S. Air Force is called in. With Clint Eastwood piloting one of the planes, the airmen firebomb the monster, saving the day.

The special effects here are quite convincing, as is the monster, "played" by a real live tarantula and "directed" by unseen air jets. When combined with the separately shot footage of the locals running in panic, the scenes of the spider on the town succeed in magnifying a common phobia to truly horrifying proportions.

Tarantula (1955)   John Agar, Leo G. Carroll, Mara Corday, Nestor Paiva, Ross Elliott, and Clint Eastwood; directed by Jack Arnold; screenplay by Robert M. Fresco and Martin Berkley, based on Fresco's teleplay "No Food for Thought"; produced by William Alland; Universal-International; 80 min. (b&w)

The local authorities make a beeline for the truck as "crawling terror 100 feet high"—to quote the movie poster—approaches in Tarantula.

"Scream for your lives," urges the announcer in the movie theater where, in crab-like fashion, The Tingler *is running amok.*

The Tingler

This spine-tingling classic hypothesizes the discovery of a crab-like parasite, the tingler, which is able to grow inside a human host when the person is overcome by fear. The only way to save oneself is to emit a primal scream, but this is almost impossible to do when one is terrified, as most moviegoers know.

Vincent Price plays the doctor who discovers the creature. A house call takes him to the apartment of a theater owner whose wife (Judith Evelyn) has succumbed to the parasite. Believing he has the perfect opportunity to research the tingler, Price obtains permission from the husband (Philip Coolidge) to operate on the corpse, little suspecting that Coolidge, in trying to scare his wife to death, was in large part responsible for her demise. The doctor does indeed find a tingler, a horrid little creature, inside her, but before it can be captured it scuttles away to terrorize the moviegoers in the theater below the apartment. In some of the film's most deliciously sinister moments, the people watching the pleasant, silent *Tol'able David* (1921) get the fright of their lives, screaming in panic as the tingler moves among them. The climax has the tingler recaptured and restored to Evelyn's dead body, whereupon it dies and the woman is reborn, leading to her husband's confession.

Schlock-meister William Castle pulled out all the stops for this one, releasing the film in a process he called Percepto. The effects included: wiring some of the seats in theaters where *The Tingler* played—to give random audience members mild electric tingles; a momentary blank screen over which it was announced that the projectionist has been killed by the tingler and viewers were told to scream for their lives; and the sudden use of color in the scene when Evelyn is frightened to death by an arm emerging from her apparently bloody bath. This sort of audience involvement eventually led to another audience participation classic, *The Rocky Horror Picture Show* (1975).

The Tingler (1959)   Vincent Price, Judith Evelyn, Philip Coolidge, Darryl Hickman, Patricia Cutts, and Pamela Lincoln; directed and produced by William Castle; screenplay by Robb White; Columbia/Castle; 82 min. (b&w with some color sequences)

(OPPOSITE) *Judith Evelyn plays a deaf mute who is frightened to death by apparitions like this one in* The Tingler.

BAD KIDS

WEIRD KIDS

Drew Barrymore is the Firestarter, *a young innocent who causes things to burst into flame when she is angered.*

Firestarter

Another Stephen King tale about a "special" kid is brought to the big screen following its stint as a best-selling novel.

This time, the heroine is a little girl (Drew Barrymore) who can start fires just by thinking about them. It's all the fault of one of those scientific experiments gone awry (the subjects were the girl's parents when in college). As the film opens, the mother is dead and the little girl and her father (David Keith) are on the run from sinister government agents who want to bring her powers under their control. The plot is rather predictable, and the distinction between the good guys and the bad guys is all too pat, but the fires are stylishly staged, each successively more grandiose, and the film holds up visually when all else falters.

Drew Barrymore of *E.T.* fame is fine as the fiery little Charlene, nicknamed Charlie, and David Keith is properly noble as her dad. But George C. Scott wears himself out as a one-eyed meanie with a silver pony tail. Other members of the generally strong cast include the always-interesting Martin Sheen, and Academy Award winners Art Carney and Louise Fletcher.

Firestarter (1984)   David Keith, Drew Barrymore, Martin Sheen, George C. Scott, Freddie Jones, Heather Locklear, Louise Fletcher, Moses Gunn, and Art Carney; directed by Mark L. Lester; screenplay by Stanley Mann, based on the Stephen King novel; produced by Frank Capra, Jr.; Universal; 115 min. (c)

(OPPOSITE) *Andy McGee (David Keith) cradles his daughter Charlie (Drew Barrymore) after government agents shoot her with a tranquilizing dart in* Firestarter.

(PREVIOUS PAGES) *Chris Udvarnoky in the moody, suggestive thriller,* The Other, *from Tom Tryon's best-selling novel. (see p. 101).*

It suddenly dawns on Nancy Kelly that her sweet, little Rhona (Patty McCormack) is evil incarnate in The Bad Seed.

The Bad Seed

Based on Maxwell Anderson's compelling stage play, this Mervyn LeRoy production features several Academy Award–nominated performances, including that of the wicked little Rhona by Patty McCormack. It's tough for a mother to suspect that her 8-year-old daughter is a liar, a cheat, and a murderess, but that's the unavoidable conclusion Rhona's mom (Nancy Kelly) must draw. When a young boy beats Rhona in a penmanship competition at school, she responds by murdering him in cold blood at the class picnic. Maintaining her innocence, Rhona is infuriated by anyone who challenges her version of events, summarily murdering them as well.

In the stage play, the child gets away with murder, an ending which the Hollywood censors of the 1950s would not allow. So instead, the film ends on an awkward, confusing note, with the play-

ers taking something akin to bows at a curtain call, and Mom taking Rhona over her knee for a well-deserved spanking. Although this hardly satisfies any viewer's need for justice, what lingers is Patty McCormack's chilling portrayal of childish evil.

The Bad Seed (1956) Nancy Kelly, Patty McCormack, Henry Jones, Eileen Heckart, Evelyn Varden, William Hopper, Paul Fix, Jesse White, Gage Clarke, Joan Croydon, and Frank Cady; directed and produced by Mervyn LeRoy; screenplay by John Lee Mahin, based on the Maxwell Anderson play of the William March novel; Warner Brothers; 127 min. (b&w)

Kiefer Sutherland is the leader of a hip group of teenage vampires in
The Lost Boys.

The Lost Boys

In its attempt to blend a hip John Hughes–like "bubble gum" picture with the tenants of a vampire film, *The Lost Boys* never really achieves lift-off, failing to emulate the best of either of the two genres.

The story finds a Phoenix mother, Lucy (Diane Wiest), and her boys, Sam (Corey Haim) and Michael (Jason Patric), moving west to Santa Carla, a California coastal town that is home to her eccentric taxidermist Dad (Barnard Hughes). In short order, each member of the newly arrived family gets involved with a sinister vampire cult. Young Sam meets the Frog brothers, comic book connoisseurs and protectors of "Truth, justice and the American way," at least as far as vampires are concerned. "Santa Carla's become a haven for the undead," says one Frog, while the other informs Sam that "ghouls and werewolves occupy high positions in city hall."

Meanwhile, Michael falls in with a strange motorcycle gang led by David (Kiefer Sutherland) and, after drinking David's blood, becomes part vampire himself. And Lucy begins to see Max (Edward Herrmann), the local video shop manager who Sam soon believes is the head vampire.

Neither truly scary nor funny, *The Lost Boys* manages to be stylish, but to little purpose. And what's worse, the film weakly employs some top acting talents who struggle through to the totally contrived happy ending.

The Lost Boys (1987) Corey Feldman, Jami Gertz, Corey Haim, Edward Herrmann, Barnard Hughes, Jason Patric, Kiefer Sutherland, and Diane Wiest; directed by Joel Schumacher; screenplay by Janice Fisher, James Jeremias, and Jeffrey Boam; produced by Harvey Bernhard; Warner Brothers; 98 min. (c)

Carrie

S tephen King's macabre novel is given new blood by director
Brian De Palma's effective staging.

Carrie (Sissy Spacek) is the mousy, somewhat backward school-
girl who is tormented by her catty classmates. As a prank, she is
nominated for prom queen, and the recognition, joke or not, helps
her to blossom. On the big night, she is, in fact, crowned queen, but
as she stands radiantly in the spotlight, she is drenched with a
bucket of pig's blood by several of her cruel classmates. Infuriated,
she exercises her awesome telekinetic powers, destroying her
school and wrecking many of the kids' cars. After the disaster of the
dance, she returns home to face her religious fanatic mother (Piper
Laurie), who believes the girl has sexually sinned. Mom actually
stabs daughter, but daughter telekinetically throws every knife in
the kitchen at mom. Not only does De Palma orchestrate a grand
apocalyptic climax, but he throws in a trick coda as well, a dream
sequence in which Carrie's bloody hand reaches out from the grave
to grab a mourner.

A blockbuster at the box office, this picture carried with it the old-
fashioned satisfaction of watching an innocent victim successfully
exact revenge. Although forgiveness may be holier, getting even is
much more fun—and more graphic! The film established both De
Palma and King in their respective fields, and furthered the careers
of a number of young actors, including John Travolta, Amy Irving,
and—most especially—Sissy Spacek.

Carrie (1976) Sissy Spacek, Piper Laurie, Amy Irving, Nancy Allen,
William Katt, John Travolta, Betty Buckley, P. J. Soles, and Sidney Lassic;
directed by Brian De Palma; screenplay by Lawrence D. Cohen, from the
novel by Stephen King; produced by Paul Monash; United Artists/Red
Bank; 98 min. (c)

*Piper Laurie is a religious fanatic who will cut the evil out of her daughter
if need be in* Carrie.

(OPPOSITE) *Drenched with pig's blood by malicious pranksters, the
telekinetic Carrie (Sissey Spacek) prepares to unleash her awesome
power on her classmates.*

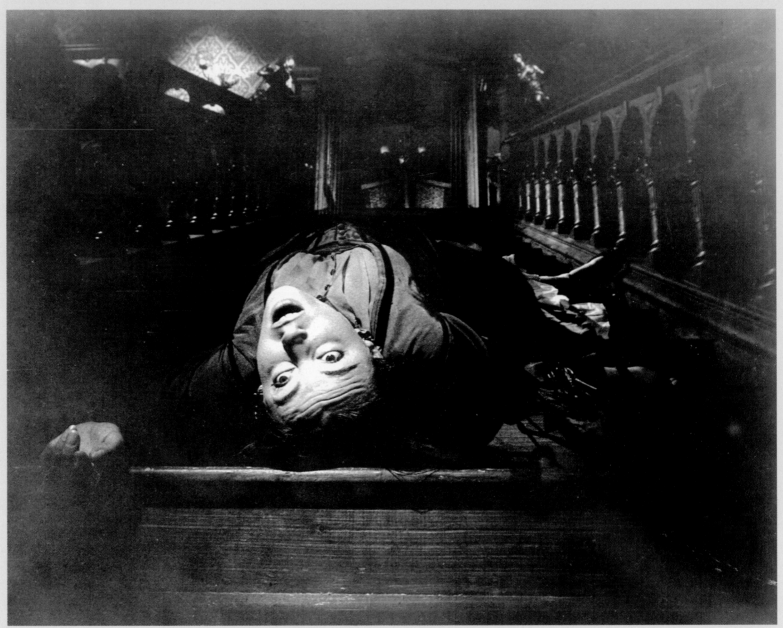

A host of evil doings at Hill House—including the unexplained death of its second mistress, Frieda Korr—draws the interest of supernatural investigators in The Haunting.

The Haunting

"Hill House, not sane, stood by itself against its hills, holding darkness within; it had stood so for eighty years … and whatever walked there, walked alone." So begins *The Haunting of Hill House*, Shirley Jackson's multifaceted 1959 novel from which the filmscript was adapted. This house is a weird old Boston mansion, with doors that pound and bulge grotesquely, spooky corridors, a snaky spiral staircase, and hardly a right angle in sight.

As the movie opens, the house is being investigated by an anthropologist, Dr. Markway (Richard Johnson), and two psychic women, one uptight (Julie Harris), the other, a lesbian (Claire Bloom). The horror comes to a head when Mrs. Markway (Lois Maxwell) arrives, sleeps in the nursery, and finds that her terror has been vicariously shared by Harris and Bloom, and that each of them has been assaulted by images of traumatic fright. The tension between the virginal Harris and the sexual Bloom gets played out in mutual clairvoyance, somewhat to Harris's discomfort.

While this film is heavy in atmosphere, it ultimately does itself in by having too many themes and by going off in too many directions. The cinematography is fancy, if not always effective, and occasionally the camera work gets in the way rather than enhancing the drama.

The Haunting (1963)   Julie Harris, Claire Bloom, Richard Johnson, Russ Tamblyn, Lois Maxwell, Fay Compton, Rosalie Crutchley, and Valentine Dyall; directed and produced by Robert Wise; screenplay by Nelson Gidding, based on the novel by Shirley Jackson; MGM/Argyle; 112 min. (b&w)

(OPPOSITE) *Julie Harris is a repressed psychic who is particularly sensitive to Hill House's unnatural emanations in* The Haunting.

(PREVIOUS PAGES) *JoBeth Williams tries to pull son Oliver Robins and daughter Dominique Dunne to safety when their room is invaded by supernatural forces in* Poltergeist *(see pp. 116-117).*

In one of The Shining's *most memorable moments, Jack Nicholson gleefully shouts "Here's Johnny!" as he tries to terrorize his wife Shelley Duvall cowering in the bathroom (see photo on pp. 2-3).*

Little Danny Lloyd puts the nonsense word "Redrum" on the door of the caretaker's apartment in The Shining. *Seen in the mirror, the word becomes "Murder."*

The Shining

With strong leading players, an accomplished director, and powerful story material, *The Shining* should have lifted horror fans to a high view of hell on earth. But Jack Nicholson's campy overacting and Stanley Kubrick's erratic direction sap the movie of its ability to shock.

The tale follows a writer (Nicholson), his wife (Shelley Duvall), and their son (Danny Lloyd) to a huge resort hotel in the Rocky Mountains where Nicholson is to serve as caretaker for the winter. Warned that a past winter caretaker got cabin fever and axed his daughters, Nicholson is blithely confident that it won't happen to him. But it does, and quite quickly he takes on the angry unpredictability of a madman. He even begins to socialize with the phantoms from the hotel's past, including its bartender and the murderous caretaker. Ultimately, the family descends into civil war, with Duvall and Lloyd fighting for their lives, and Nicholson determined to recreate the familial axe murder. The heroic, "happy" ending has a distant hotel cook (Scatman Crothers) use his psychic powers ("the shining") to check on fellow psychic Lloyd, and then provide the snowcat that enables mother and son to escape. Along the way, there are moments that illustrate Kubrick's undeniable directorial skill: the repeated use of Danny riding his tricycle through the endless hallways, the quick cuts to the axe-murdered daughters, and the slow-motion elevator opening to an ocean of blood.

Still, Stephen King, who wrote the novel, wasn't too thrilled with the result. "Neither Stanley Kubrick nor his screenwriter Diane Johnson had any knowledge of the genre," the novelist complained. "It was like they had never seen a horror movie before, so they did a lot of things audiences had seen before."

The Shining (1980) Jack Nicholson, Shelley Duvall, Danny Lloyd, Scatman Crothers, Barry Nelson, Phillip Stone, and Joe Turkel; directed and produced by Stanley Kubrick; screenplay by Stanley Kubrick and Diane Johnson, based on the novel by Stephen King; Warner Brothers; 146 min. (c)

A Mixed Brew

The House of Usher *falls—literally—as Roderick (Vincent Price) and his sister Madeline (Myrna Fahey) perish and the mansion crumbles into a black swamp.*

House of Usher

This stylish remake of a classic Poe story established filmmaker Roger Corman as a serious artist and led to a series of Poe films including *The Pit and the Pendulum* and *The Raven*. Known for his ability to produce credible horror films over a weekend at under $100,000, Corman used his relatively luxurious $200,000 budget and three-week shooting schedule to good advantage in creating this haunting examination of a man's heart of darkness.

Under the spell of a family curse, Roderick Usher (Vincent Price) fears for the sanity of his sister Madeline (Myrna Fahey), so he entrances her and buries her alive. But Madeline refuses to stay 6 feet under and, with bloody fingers, claws her way out of the coffin. Gaunt and ghostly, somewhere between life and death, she stalks her brother to exact revenge. But love and passion are still the dominant chords between them, and she is powerless to spread her taste of death. Sputtering toward an agonizing end, she clings to her brother, even as the House of Usher itself splits in two, to sink into a

black swamp amid streaks of lightning.

Corman's *House of Usher* marked a new trend within the genre, harkening back to Gothic horror, and to stories in which human madness, rather than monsters, aliens, or supernatural beings served as the demon.

House of Usher (1960)   Vincent Price, Mark Damon, Myrna Fahey, Harry Ellerbe, Bill Borzage, and Mike Jordan; directed and produced by Roger Corman; screenplay by Richard Matheson, based on the story by Edgar Allan Poe; American International Pictures; 85 min. (c)

(OPPOSITE) *With* The House of Usher, *starring Vincent Price, horrormaster Roger Corman "ushered" in a series of movies based on tales of Edgar Allen Poe.*

(PREVIOUS PAGES) *Adrienne Barbeau is a nagging wife who is about to become an ancient monster's supper in* Creepshow *(see pp. 136-137).*

Though charred beyond recognition, the undaunted Chucky keeps on coming, much to Catherine Hicks's horror in Child's Play.

Child's Play

This creepy thriller manages to find horror in a most unlikely source: a 3-foot-tall red-haired toy that can speak several stock phrases, such as "Hi, I like to be hugged!" and "Hi, I'm Chucky, your friend to the end."

Indeed, it's a happy day when young Andy Barclay (Alex Vincent) gets his talking "Good Guy" doll, but joy soon turns to terror when the child is hospitalized in a psychiatric ward for possibly committing two murders, including that of his babysitter. But the murderer isn't Andy. It's Chucky, actually a serial killer who has transferred his soul to the doll. Determined to escape the confines of his inanimate body, the doll decides to take over the form of little Andy.

Good performances by Catherine Hicks and Alex Vincent as mother and son give the film credibility. Strong scripting keeps the villainous Chucky—the *real* Chucky, as opposed to his doll-like performance—offscreen until the film has built up a head of steam. And when the evil doll does take center stage, the effect is truly sin-

ister. In a fight to the finish between Chucky, Andy, Mom, and a detective friend (Chris Sarandon), Chucky is burned alive, clubbed, and shot, and still his charred parts keep on coming. What a doll!

Child's Play (1988)   Catherine Hicks, Chris Sarandon, Alex Vincent, Brad Dourif, and Dinah Manoff; directed by Tom Holland; screenplay by Don Mancini, John Lafia, and Tom Holland; produced by David Kirschner; United Artists; 88 min. (c)

(OPPOSITE) *Who wouldn't want a doll like Chucky in* Child's Play? *After all, he promises to be "your friend to the end."*

Christine is a 1958 Plymouth Fury that doesn't take kindly to fender benders, as this terrified teen is about to discover.

Christine

This Stephen King yarn about a killer car had a lot of miles on it when John Carpenter decided to gas it up for another run. The title character is a '58 Plymouth Fury—and once this baby's fury is engaged, everyone else better get off the road.

Keith Gordon plays the car's owner, whose personality is transformed by the vehicle's unabashed mayhem. Passing quickly from nerd to obnoxious cad, Gordon takes great pleasure in the revenge he's able to wreak, with Christine as his alter ego. The car does a bit of revenge wreaking on its own as well. After Gordon's enemies bash the car with sledgehammers, the vehicle magically reassembles itself and then hunts each of them down. This four-wheeled mayhem is designed to give audiences the same kind of satisfaction that they found in King's Carrie, when the heroine telekinetically destroys her enemies, but the teenager in that earlier work is a lot more sympathetic than Christine.

The film's climax comes when Gordon's girlfriend (Alexandra Paul) and best buddy (John Stockwell) attempt to save their pal by destroying the car. Though Christine is eventually compacted, it seems likely that someway, somehow, this malevolent roadster will be on the road again.

Christine (1983)   Keith Gordon, Alexandra Paul, John Stockwell, Robert Prosky, Harry Dean Stanton, and Christine Belford; directed by John Carpenter; screenplay by Bill Phillips, based on the novel by Stephen King; produced by Richard Kobrits; Columbia/Delphi Productions; 110 min. (c)

The Picture of Dorian Gray

Director Albert Lewin penned this adaptation of Oscar Wilde's penetrating novel, which focuses on a vain man (Hurd Hatfield) who manages to stay young while his portrait clearly shows signs of his debauchery and his heinous crimes. The tension in the movie lies in seeing whether or not he can retain his youth—and his wicked ways—perpetually. Harry Stradling won an Academy Award for his cinematography, and this is his picture as much as the director's. In a bold dramatic stroke, Lewin chooses to reveal the horridly aged and blood-bespattered painted portrait at the end of the film in color, while shooting the principal portion of the story in black and white. This deft use of the medium gives the movie's climax punch and depth, showing the audience quite clearly the results of Dorian Gray's perversity.

Strong performances by the leading players endow the movie with the solidity such a dour subject deserves. Particular standouts are George Sanders as Lord Wootton, the jaded tempter, and Angela Lansbury as the ingenue songstress. In only her third film, Lansbury received her second Oscar nomination.

The Picture of Dorian Gray (1945)   Hurd Hatfield, George Sanders, Angela Lansbury, Peter Lawford, Donna Reed, and Miles Mander; directed and written by Albert Lewin, based on the novel by Oscar Wilde; produced by Pandro S. Berman; MGM; 110 min. (b&w with some color sequences)

(OPPOSITE) The Picture of Dorian Gray portrays a depraved cad (Hurd Hatfield) who stays young and handsome while his portrait becomes a reflection of his true nature.

The Little Shop of Horrors, *Roger Corman's comic tale of a man-eating plant, was filmed in two days.*

The Little Shop of Horrors

This is surely the wittiest comic horror story ever filmed in two days. Delighted by the reception of *A Bucket of Blood* (1959), his macabre comedy shot in five days, Roger Corman set out to top himself and did so, in every way.

The plot centers around a plant store in the seedy part of town, run by the nauseating Gravis Mushnik and his nudnick employee, Seymour Krelboin, who's in love with Mushnik's daughter, Audrey. Seymour can't marry Audrey till he supplies his hypochondriac mother with an iron lung, and toward that end he creates a radical new plant, a cross between a butterwort and a Venus's-flytrap. This bizarre vegetable, which Seymour lovingly names Audrey, Jr., speaks in a male voice and has a voracious appetite—for people. "Feed me! Feed me!" cries the plant. "I want some chow!" But not just any chow, Seymour finds out, for though the plant savors gunmen, it regurgitates their guns with a belch. A delightful subplot features a sadistic dentist. "Hurt?" he asks, as he indiscriminately drills a patient's tooth. "Good, you ain't felt nothing yet!" But the dentist meets his match when he works on masochist Wilbur Force, a man who reads *Pain* magazine and goes to the dentist for kicks. Reveling in the part, the young Jack Nicholson eschews painkiller: "No novocaine," he insists, "it dulls the senses."

In 1982, a reworked *Little Shop* opened as a hit off-Broadway musical, and this was subsequently turned into a highly successful film, directed—in more than two days—by Frank Oz.

The Little Shop of Horrors (1960) Jonathan Haze, Jackie Joseph, Mel Welles, Myrtle Vail, Dick Miller, and Jack Nicholson; directed and produced by Roger Corman; screenplay by Charles B. Griffith; Santa Clara/Filmgroup; 70 min. (b&w)

In the musical remake of The Little Shop of Horrors *(1986), the plant, Audrey II, becomes "a mean, green mother from outer space" with the voice of Four Tops singer Levi Stubbs.*

In The Island of Dr. Moreau *(1977), Michael York, seen here at left, is turned from human to humanoid when he tries to interfere with the mad doctor's work.*

Island of Lost Souls

An exciting adaptation of H. G. Wells's startling novel *The Island of Dr. Moreau*, this film had American audiences astir in the 1930s, and was not allowed to be released in Great Britain until 1958.

Charles Laughton as the hyped-up mad scientist Dr. Moreau is banished from England because of his cruel experiments on dogs. Settling in on a remote tropical island (actually Catalina Island off the California coast), the mad doctor begins his experiments in earnest, attempting to transform animals into humanoids. Through bizarre surgical grafts between humans and animals, he succeeds in creating a ragtag race of mongrels, which he keeps in line with a

At the climax of Island of Lost Souls, *the humanoid creations of Dr. Moreau (Charles Laughton) turn on their "benefactor."*

whip and frequent hypnotic chanting. His principal henchman is "humanimal" Bela Lugosi, who constantly tries to repress his animal nature by chanting: "Not to eat meat. . . . Not to chase other men. . . . Not to go on all fours. . . . Not to gnaw the bark off trees. . . . That is the Law!"

Dr. Moreau begins to work on his plan to mate a human with a beautiful woman he converted from a panther (presaging the 1942 *Cat People*). But all the doctor's plans come undone when he incites the now tame Lugosi to kill for him, and at the climax it is Dr. Moreau himself who is dragged into his House of Pain for some radical surgery.

Remade as *The Island of Dr. Moreau* in 1977, the new color version lacks the foreboding of Karl Struss's original black-and-white cinematography. And though Burt Lancaster and Michael York are fine actors, they don't come up to the menace of Laughton and Lugosi.

Island of Lost Souls (1932) Charles Laughton, Bela Lugosi, Richard Arlen, Kathleen Burke, Leila Hyams, and Alan Ladd; directed by Erle C. Kenton; screenplay by Waldemar Young, from the novel by H. G. Wells; Paramount; 72 min. (b&w)

Stephen King, the master of the modern horror novel and screenwriter of Creepshow, *plays a man turning into a fungus in one of the film's episodes.*

Creepshow

An homage to the grisly *E.C.* comic books of the 1950s, *Creepshow* is a five-story horror anthology by masters of the macabre, George Romero and Stephen King. The film opens with an angry father throwing his son's ghoulish *E.C.* comics into the trash. A gusty wind blows open the pages, and the film switches to animation, a style that serves as the introduction to each episode.

In "Father's Day," a murdered patriarch (John Amplas) returns from the grave to claim his birthday cake. Author Stephen King stars in the second story, "The Lonesome Death of Jordy Verill," playing a dopey backwoods farmer who gets transformed into a fungus after breaking open a meteorite in the hopes of finding riches. In "Something to Tide You Over," a vengeful husband (Leslie Neilsen) buries his wife and her lover up to their necks in beach sand as the tide rolls in. "The Crate" features Hal Holbrook as a college professor who gets rid of his nagging wife (Adrienne Barbeau) by feeding her to a 150-year-old Arctic ghoul, set free for the occasion. *Creepshow* closes, appropriately, with "They're Creeping Up on You," in which E. G. Marshall plays an eccentric millionaire with a cleanliness fetish whose worst fears come true when his penthouse is invaded by hordes of cockroaches. The insects swarm over the apartment and ultimately into Marshall's nose, ears, and mouth.

Stephen King called *Creepshow* "basically a junk food movie, but high-class junk food," and with its strong leading players and occasionally creepy sequences, the film lives up to his billing. A sequel, *Creepshow 2*, was released in 1987 and featured three more King tales, minus the comic book and animated intros.

Creepshow (1982)   Hal Holbrook, Adrienne Barbeau, Viveca Lindfors, Carrie Nye, E. G. Marshall, Leslie Neilsen, Fritz Weaver, and Stephen King; directed by George Romero; screenplay by Stephen King; produced by Richard Romero; Warner Brothers; 122 min. (c)

The host of Creepshow *looks particularly attractive in the moonlight.*

INDEX

The look of horror—Lee Remick in The Omen.